A Guide to Stuff You

Contents

Sea shells ... ... Pages 1 to 26
Other sea animals ... ... Pages 27 to 38
Seaweeds ... ... Pages 39 to 42
Pebbles ... ... Pages 43 to 46
Glossary of useful words ... Page 47

Common cockle

Cerastoderma edule

Cockles can grow to 5cm across. Their shells may be white, pale brown or greyish. They live buried in sand, mud or muddy gravel. They filter food from sea water (they are filter feeders).

> These shells are in a nursery rhyme... but which one?

Pod razor shell

Ensis siliqua

Pod razors are long, thin and shiny shells which are crunchy under your wellies. They live deep under the sand and they are filter feeders. There are several other kinds of razors. Some have slightly curved shells.

Common mussel
Myrtilus edulis

Common mussels can grow up to 10cm long, but they are usually smaller than this. Young mussel shells are brownish. Mussels live together in beds fixed onto rocks. They filter their food from the sea water.

Horse mussel
Modiolus modiolus

Horse mussel shells are up to 14cm long. They live together in reefs on the sea bed. They also filter food from sea water.

> Horse mussel shells are much larger, and have a more rounded tip, than common mussels.

4

Variegated scallop
Chlamys varia

Variegated scallop shells have 25 to 35 ribs on them and are slightly taller than they are wide. They are filter feeders. They live on sand or gravel.

> Variegated and queen scallops can swim under water. They do it by quickly opening and shutting their shells like castanets!

Queen scallop
Aequipecten opercularis

Queen scallops (or 'queenies') are more rounded than variegated scallops, and have only about 20 ribs on their shell. They also live on sandy or gravelly areas of the sea bed and are filter feeders as well.

Thick trough shell
Spisula solida

Thick trough shells can be up to 5cm in size. Their shells are very heavy and strong. Thick trough shells live under the sand and they filter food from sea water.

> Another name for these shells is 'surf clams'.

Rayed trough shell
Mactra stultorum

Rayed trough shells also reach 5cm across. Their shells are not as heavy as thick trough shells, they are smoother and are decorated with a pattern of faint rays. They are sand-dwelling filter feeders.

Pullet carpet shell
Venerupis senegalensis

Pullet carpet shells grow up to 5cm in width. Their home is under sand or gravel and they are another example of a filter feeder.

> Pullet carpet shells sometimes have pretty patterns of rays or zigzags.

Common oyster
Ostrea edulis

Common oysters have one flat and one cupped shell. They reach 10cm across. Oysters live on the surface of sand, mud or gravel and are filter feeding animals. The shells are cream, brown or greyish.

Thin tellin

Angulus tenuis

Thin tellins are pretty pink, pale yellow or white shells that are quite flat and very delicate. They can grow up to 3cm across. They live under the sand and get their food by filtering sea water.

Baltic tellin
Macoma balthica

Baltic tellin shells are stronger and more cupped than thin tellins, reaching 2 to 3cm in size. They live in a similar way to thin tellins.

Baltic tellins look like babies' finger-nails, but they can be white as well as pink.

White piddock
Barnea candida

White piddocks live inside a hole which they drill into chalk, peat, clay or wood. Their fragile shells look like angel wings, and grow to 6cm long. They are yet another example of a filter feeding animal.

American rock borer

Petricola pholadiformis

American rock borers are like white piddocks except that their shells are thicker, and at the rock borer's hinge (shown by the arrow), there are 2 or 3 little teeth.

> Look for the hinge teeth on the rock borer to tell it and the piddock apart.

14

Blunt gaper
Mya truncata

Blunt gapers have rough shells up to 7cm long. One side of the shell is turned upwards slightly, giving the shell a straight edge. Blunt gapers' home is in sand or muddy sand and they filter food from sea water.

Common winkle
Littorina littorea

Common winkles can be purple, reddish-brown, grey or black and they grow up to 2cm tall. Winkles live amongst rocks and on mudflats and their food is tiny seaweeds.

> Winkles love eating sea lettuce (page 41).

16

Flat periwinkle
Littorina obtusata

Flat periwinkles have colourful yellow, orange or green shells that are smooth and very thick. They live on rocks amongst seaweed, and they eat seaweed.

> Flat periwinkles only grow to just over 1cm tall.

Necklace shell
Euspira species

Necklace shells (or 'moon snails') are brownish and smooth. Underneath the shell, next to its entrance, there is a little hole in the middle. Necklace shells drill holes in other shells and eat the animals inside.

Common whelk
Buccinum undatum

Common whelks grow up to 11cm tall and have many ridges on their shell. Whelks live on the sea bed and their food is worms, shellfish and dead sea animals.

> Whelk shells that spiral in the opposite direction to normal are extremely rare.

Dog whelk
Nucella lapillus

Dog whelks are cream or yellow, up to 3cm tall. Their shells are smoother and thicker than common whelks. Their home is on rocks, amongst the barnacles and mussels which they eat.

Sting winkle
Ocenebra erinacea

Sting winkles (also called 'oyster drills') grow up to 6cm tall and have a rough and knobbly shell. They live on rocks and under stones. They drill into oyster shells and suck out all the meat.

Cowrie
Trivia species

Cowries are egg shaped, have a slit underneath and reach 1cm long. Their shells are small and hard to find. Their home is amongst rocks and they eat soft bodied animals called sea squirts.

Big cowrie shells from tropical countries were used in schools for learning counting.

Grey topshell
Gibbula cineraria

Grey topshells have fine purply-brown bands on them. Old shells are often partly worn through and are pearly. They reach 1cm tall and live amongst seaweed. They eat tiny seaweeds.

> Their pearly tops mean these shells are also called 'silver Tommies'.

Painted topshell
Calliostoma zizyphinum

Painted topshells are cone shaped shells that can either have pink markings or be plain white. They grow up to 3cm tall. They live in similar habitats to grey topshells, and they eat seaweeds and also small animals.

Common limpet
Patella vulgata

Common limpets are cone shaped shells that grow up to 3cm tall. They are greyish-green on the inside, but this colour is worn away on old shells. Common limpets feed by filing away at seaweeds growing on rocks.

Slipper limpet
Crepidula fornicata

Slipper limpets have a white shelf on the underside of their shell. They live together on top of each other in stacks in oyster and mussel beds. They are filter feeders up to 5cm long.

> Slipper limpets originally came from North America.

Cuttlefish bone
Sepia officinalis

A cuttlefish bone (or cuttlebone) comes from inside an animal closely related to an octopus. Cuttlebones may be as long as 20cm. When they get washed up on the beach, they are often pecked at by birds.

People buy pieces of cuttlebone for their pet budgies.

Crab shell

The shell or claws of green shore crabs, harbour crabs and edible crabs can be found on beaches. They may not be from a dead crab. Crabs have to shed their old shell from time to time so they can grow bigger.

Mermaid's purses

Mermaid's purses are empty egg-cases laid by dogfish, skates or rays. They can be black or brown. It is possible to identify which kind of fish laid them based on their size and shape. Each one contained a single baby fish.

Whelk's egg-cases

Whelk's egg-cases look like screwed up balls of tough, brown bubblewrap. After the baby whelks hatch out, the egg-case is lighter and washes up on the beach.

> These are also called 'sea wash balls' because sailors used them for scrubbing.

Green sea urchin
Psammechinus miliaris

Green sea urchin 'tests' (shells) are circular and up to 5cm in diameter. They live under rocks and amongst seaweed, which is their food.

Living green sea urchins are protected by lots of sharp, green spines. These eventually drop off after the animal dies.

Sea potato
Echinocardium cordatum

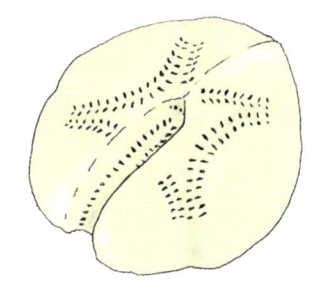

A sea potato is the 'test' of an animal called a heart urchin. They are very thin, fragile and easy to break. Heart urchins live under sand, and eat small pieces of food that they collect from amongst the sand.

Common starfish

Asterias rubens

Common starfish are orange and have 5 arms. These starfish often live on mussel beds. They eat several kinds of creatures, and can force apart shells with their strong arms to eat the animal inside.

Moon jellyfish
Aurelia aurita

Moon jellyfish live in the open sea but can be found washed up on the beach, sometimes in large numbers. On fresh specimens you can see a circle pattern in the middle of their 'bell'.

Don't touch! Some jellyfish can sting.

Hornwrack
Flustra folicacea

Hornwrack is tough, papery and bushy. It looks like a seaweed but is a colony of lots of tiny animals called zooids. It grows on shells or stones.

Hornwrack is also called 'amberweed'. It washes up at the top of the beach in the same places as amber (page 46).

Sea firs

There are several different kinds of sea firs. Common ones are pale brown, slightly shiny and look like little trees. They are made of lots of tiny animals like sea anemones, which collect food from the water.

Keel worm tubes

Pomatoceros species

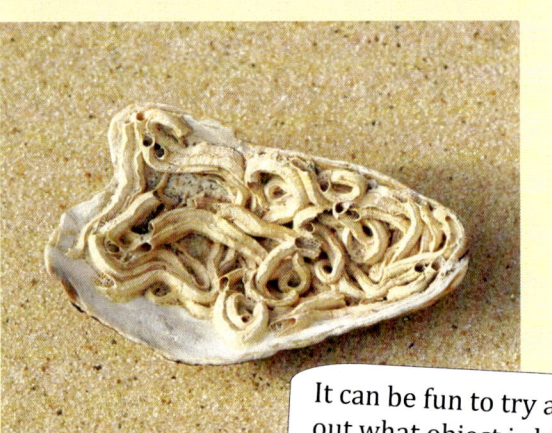

Keel worm tubes are white, cream or grey, hard and thin. They look like spaghetti and are fixed onto shells and stones. The worms that lived inside the tubes collected food from sea water.

> It can be fun to try and work out what object is hidden under big lumps of keel worm tubes.

Sponge

Pieces of sponge feel rubbery when wet, light when dry, and are full of little holes. Different kinds can be like fat blobs or long, thin fingers. Sponges live under the sea fixed onto rocks and they are filter feeders.

Some seaweeds you can find

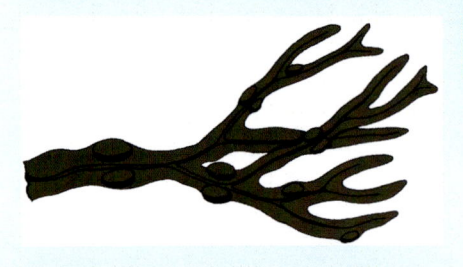

Bladder wrack *Fucus vesiculosus*

This seaweed has air bladders often in pairs, a smooth edge to the fronds and an obvious midrib.

Knotted or egg wrack
Ascophyllum nodosum

Single large air bladders in middle of fronds. No midrib.

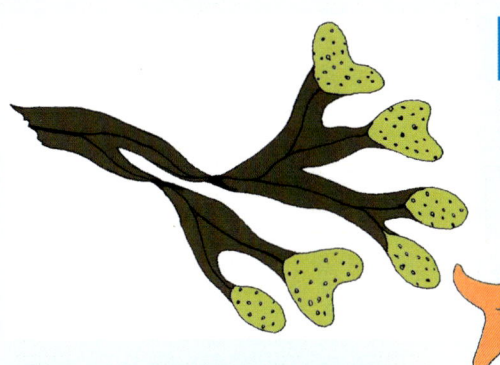

Spiral wrack *Fucus spiralis*

The fronds are twisted. It has no air bladders, but does have an obvious midrib.

The pale green blobs at the end of spiral wrack fronds will produce spores that grow into new seaweeds.

Toothed wrack
Fucus serratus

No air bladders. Saw-tooth edge to fronds. Big midrib.

Sea lettuce *Ulva lactuca*

Sea lettuce is translucent and looks like pieces of green plastic bag. Sea lettuce washed up on the beach has sometimes been torn to shreds by the rough waves.

Red seaweeds

Red seaweeds are often very beautiful, but on the beach it can be difficult to tell what they are. Float a piece in sea water to see how delicate the fronds are. This feathery red seaweed was pressed and carefully mounted on paper by a Victorian naturalist.

42

Some pebbles you can find

Most pebbles on East Anglian beaches, and in the photo opposite, are **Flint**. Flint is bluish-grey, black or brown.

Sea glass (SG on the photo) is green, brown or white and is from old broken bottles. When dry, the surface looks frosted.

Milky quartz (MQ) pebbles are snow white, hard and smooth. Quartz with pink or yellowish markings can be found too.

Jasper (J) is a beautiful smooth, red, opaque stone.

Carnelian (C) pebbles are translucent, orange to red, smooth and slightly shiny. Carnelian is a rare, semi-precious stone.

People used to think that flints with holes in were lucky. These stones were hung on strings near doorways to protect the home against witches.

Carnelian is best found by searching areas of wet pebbles with the sun in front of you.

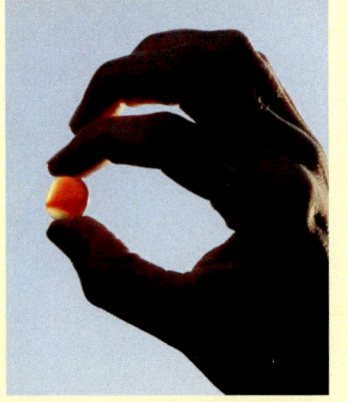

This pebble was from chalk that had been drilled by piddocks or rock borers (pages 13 & 14).

Chalk pebbles (picture above) are creamy-white and have a pitted surface. Chalk is a soft rock.

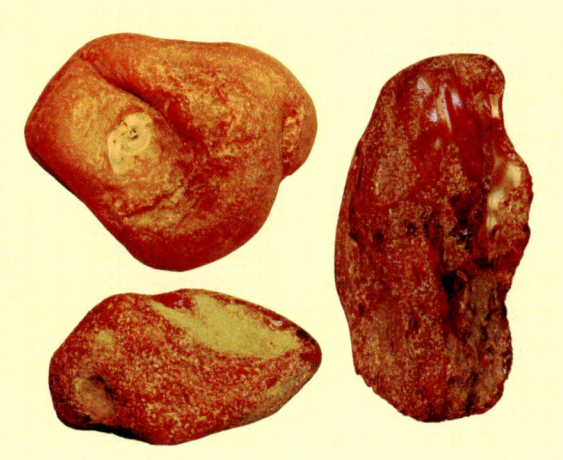

Amber

Amber is fossil resin from ancient pine trees and is 40 million years old. East Anglian beaches are the best places in Britain for finding pieces of amber.

Amber feels light and warm to the touch. After it has been polished, it can be translucent and roughly the colour of golden syrup, or opaque and the colour of toffee. Amber is rare and valuable. It is used for jewellery or carvings.

Glossary of Useful Words

Colony. Lots of minute animals living together as one unit.
Air bladder. Hollow bumps on some seaweeds that help them to float.
Filter feeder. An animal which sucks in sea water, and then sieves out tiny plants or animals for food. Many sea animals are filter feeders.
Habitat. The place where a plant or animal lives.
Midrib. A large, thick vein running down the middle of a seaweed frond (or a leaf).
Opaque. Something that does not let light through.
Semi-precious stone. Rare and beautiful stones that can be used to make jewellery. They are not as valuable as precious stones like diamonds and rubies.
Test. Special name for the shell of a sea urchin.
Translucent. Light shines through translucent things, but you cannot see clearly through them.